Sighs and Stray Gusts and Other Occasional Poems

Sighs and Stray Gusts and Other Occasional Poems
Frank Praeger

DEADMAN PUBLISHING

Houghton, Michigan
2016

Published by Dead Man Publishing, LLC
Copyright © 2016 by Frank Praeger
All Rights Reserved.

ISBN 978-0-9827014-3-0

Dead Man Publishing, LLC
400 Agate Street
Houghton, MI 49931

Library of Congress Control Number: 2016956346

Acknowledgements

ABRIDGED(UK):"Unconstrained In or Out of Season"
ANASTOMOO(AU):"Sighs and Stray Gusts"
BOGG:"Looking"
BOLTS OF SILK(UK) :"Throw Aways"
CARTYS POETRY JOURNAL(Ireland):"Exuberant"
CURLEW(UK):"Who Else Is Indolent"
DECANTO(UK):"Jade"
ENVOI(UK):"Remembering Some Verses by Pablo Neruda",
"After
Looking at a Drawing by Albrecht Durer",
FINE MADNESS:"A Sometime Curmudgeon Spells Out His
Brief"
FLAMING ARROWS(Ireland):"3/22/03"
LOOKOUT(UK):"Continent After Continent"
MID-JUNE:"Trees, Too","Thankless Summons","Gouged","The
Pitiless Complained"
PITTSBURGH QUARTERLY:"Travelling the Back Roads of the
Keweenaw"
POETRY MONTHLY(UK):"Approaching My Sixty-third Birthday",
"Last August","Synecdoche"
POTOMAC REVIEW: "On the Intertidal Rocks"
POTPOURRI: "Corona, Calyx, Spathe","This Leafing Surges"
PULSAR POETRY(UK):"Aong Others, Teddybears"
QUANTUM LEAP(UK): "Late Autumn"
RE:AL: "Milkweed and Roses"
STAND(UK): "Anonymous","Turtle Pond"
THE JOURNAL(UK):"Me! Me! Me!","Normal"
THE SEVENTH QUARRY(UK):"A Day's Message"
TIGHT: "Leveller","Walking Out","Winter in the Keweenaw",
"Mid..."

CONTENTS

ONE

TWO

THREE

ONE

Who Else Is Indolent

For Betzi, Kate, and Kraig

Joined, still to choppy blue

      to changing green

to leaves, wind
varying
reflected light

      to a red-winged black bird.

Who else is indolent? Who saunters by my side
picking raspberries, thimbleberries, sugarplums?
At the summit,
who scans the horizon for Isle Royale?

Today, the raptors are invisible.
Today, the wind comes in from nowhere, the horizonal haze
immeasurable. Today, we are floating above the lake,
trafficking in blueberries and hazel nuts,
bending with the wind on a precipice,
having come here to the dwarf oaks, the juniper,
the far away falling away,
and the relief -

noises in the distance.

We pause, looking up from our foraging,

half-hidden among bushes and dwarf trees.

This Leafing Surges

This leafing surges,
this greening, blueing, flowering

surges,
    purple, yellow, white,
surges,
    sepal dappling, leaf cusped, overlapping profluence,
emerges,
    blossom, pollen -
feculent, fragrant -
emerges,
    stamen, pistil, petal fused,
bracted into spathe,
spikey inflorescencing,
light captured, light reflecting coruscated entrances,
angled angles, myriaded juxtapositions
of leafing, branching, flowering,
frenetic fragrancing -

surges,

contained of unrepetitive,
                branchy,
                    bladed...,
petal by petal,
unveined by veined leaf - untrumpeted, cacophonous -

surging,

undiddling

throughout each last glint's gleam.

Late Autumn

Days,
light,
faces
fade.
Clouds

and cold rain;
woods

and wandering;
snow

and slush,
slipping

in the mud.
The last few apples,
the last of anything...
dead deer tied to the top of cars,
tied, hauled off -
grey sky, grey water -
opaque, dulled, greying matter.

Day follows day;
clouds
crowd. . .
devoid of leaves
bushes bristle
stand
on stand.

Hold!

Only distance goes.

Chickadees pause,
one flies.

Two intertwined trees moan.

A bluejay lights.

A squirrel,
          standing,
                    scolds.

Winter in the Keweenaw

Snow

undulating,
and light
dim, then... then brightening,
and glare

reflected, reflecting and

undulated
and,

everywhere,
surfaces
dissolving, reappearing,
surfaces
shadowing and shadowed,
smooth,
and blued:

snow   drifting over snow,
wind-driven,
drifting   across rock,

shrub,

road.

Mid...

Mid-winter,
mid-spring,

willows,
bared,
bear -

shoots, yellow
with sap,

flare.

The horizontal hovers:
purpled hazed hills,
vagaries of form -
filigreed out of trees,

                red glints,

                        dull orange.

Crows cross
settling in on the tallest Lombardy poplar
waiting for dissolution -

consumed,

eaten -

waiting for each other.

Travelling the Back Roads of the Keweenaw

Black decimated,
gold,
trunk and leaves
lichen splotched
converge.
Gold matted, arced, subtended...
silhouettes flicker;
flung shadows charge the fields,
dissemble -
partitioned...
partitioned self.

Should have been,
should have been as altered thickets,
as pileated fallen trees,
surprised grouse flagelating air,
that ever penultimate shrilling of a cricket,
its ever diminuendo...

ever inconstant...

ever distant....

Should have been as the chary squirrel leaps,
as, tumultuously, leaves reconfigure;

or not to have been,
not to have been entangled,
not discontinuous,
dismembered -
gold slashed on black,
cold
edgeless,
gloam
sempiternal.

An inner eye weeps.

...what should have been...
...could have been seen....

The earth protrudes.
Yellow withers.

Great leaves slacken.

The light thinner.

Landscape,
            everywhere,
                    threatened.

Trees, Too

Trees, too, are stubborn,
refuse to yield.
Why not walk upright among them,
why not walk over pine needles,
why not be wreathed in branches,
be autumnal diminishment,
expose unnoticed chromophores,
segregate stubble, brown bracken,
relinquish yearnings, separate twig from twig,
why not -
why not be color, self, be yearning?
Pine needles soften, loose feathers
scurry over the edge.
Why not be tatter, falter, tear?
Yes, be furthered.
Yes, capture
pine needle, loosened feather,
chapped skin, diminished color;
yes to root snarled, footfall,
gestural tree limbs -
the many eyes watchful.
Or warble, decipher each to the other.
To-wit-to-woo, to be pursued,
crossed over, hexed,
pictographed into self!

No one we can not recognize
walks beside us,
no rot, no swollen aegis.

Willard will be, will be...,
whoever turns...,

nematodes,

worms.

...and who mounted no horse.
This day, the sky is cloudless,
wind

frozen.

Normal

Two fuchsia blooms in a dish of water, antenna-like stamen,
curled petals, yellow, yellow-orange, on
a semi-circular table
in an enclosed porch
with a lilac branch scratching a window pane,
one open window - no further description
or sudden seizure, no intensification of light
or bell shaped curve to huddle in.
Two cats retreat from under the car,
watch from a distance.
A chipmunk's hindlegs, backside, tail remain.
Was it the one who followed my wife
as she watered the garden?

I hear little.

Something grows in my ear.

I feel no pain.

Dust rises with each footstep.

The sky's pellucid,
an apparent transparency that offers nothing.

I'm in an unexplainable landscape.

Any day now we expect rain.

Corona, Calyx, Spathe

I never did
imagine flowers, plants -
impassioned, caught up with,
never
the leaves, the petals, sepals,
never
ensnared by petal,
stammering over pistil, stamen,
never was
perceived as inner whorl,
corona,
never gilded depth,
imagined calyx, spathe,
resplendent folds of yellow,
of red
speckled, blotched black-purple,
orange shock, orange checkered
with blue, with yellow,
never

was drizzle,
leaf tipped,
never bee
anther touching, pollen dusted,
never fragrance
transmitted,
never
bee hunger,
never
butterfly driven,
never
pistiled, stamened,
never
wanting other
than soil,
than sun,

than water,

nor happy
imagining never having been
foxglove,
bluebell, painted daisy,
never having been
driven to fragrance, color,
to purple, pink,

to lavender,
never
having been

driven to flower.

Milkweed and Roses

Milkweed and roses, butterflies
joined end to end;
the topmost lifts off, lifting the two of them,
resettles on a further milkweed blossom;
the bottommost starts slowly fanning its wings, once,
twice.
My nose approaches; end to end, again,
the butterflies lift off,
fragrance covering me,
them,
as thimbleberries ripen, apples stir,
insects stare.

Mesmerized,
carefully,

lengthily,

inhaling air,
my nose abutting clustered milkweed blossoms, fragrance
diffusing past immediacy, the just passed stonewall,
rosebushes,   irrecoverable roses' scent,
past my myopic vision, past the winged darting
yellow-black bumblebees,
edifices, immanent intimations...,
past any purported incarnidine

       trumpeted
              prophet's abyss,...

straightening up, back through the underbrush,
onto the path, each footstep stirring up dust....

Disturbances, droppings -
how quiet it all is.

How unobtrusive sunlight.

How residual,   how final
the barely present present.
How early,
                    how late.

Milkweed and roses,   bumblebees and butterflies
straitlaced,
still,

quietly copulating.

Turtle Pond

Towards Turtle pond,
down an ORV enlarged dirt path,
wild pink scattered under bladder campion;
a chickadee's call interspersed with a crow's.
A bull frog's unlocalized croak floating across the water,
thimbleberry blooming beside the pond, the turtles missing,
their favorite half-sunk log,
protruding in the middle of the pond, unoccupied.
Sugarplums coloring burnt red.
A ruffed grouse whirrs away - 6 feet away.
A white admiral, a mourning cloak - maybe.
Two orange butterflies mating in mid flight.
Fritillaries or monarchs or viceroys.

And of the others,
a counting frenzy gets nowhere,
reminders of a haunted earth,
cries that know nothing of despair.

The wavering
              distance-making

                    slowed stridulation of a cricket

accompanies me on the way homeward

5/20/93

Shaken,
seized,
willless, willful;
flutings for the forgotten,
the unremembered;
transience huddling knee deep in self,
knee deep in droppings.

The visible contends -
air gleaming gold,
splotched drunken dried blue folding,
unfolding.

Paired ambivalences skim -
seized,
          shaken.
And the wind...
and the way forward?
Gold
        flashing, blue
                        zigzagging,
aery furtivenesses,
those moving edges, darkened centers.

And who 's forsaken,
who shelterless?

Sudden
golden immolations.
Seized,

shaken.

TWO

Synecdoche

Light stays at the frontdoor entrance,
it does not come in.
No matter morning's brightness
I and my small fingers are more concerned
with how to delicately, patiently, peel away
my mother's sunburnt, near-transparent, desiccated skin.

Nearly seventy years - sixty since I last saw her.
There was a gravel driveway, privet,
an open door, maybe, a spaniel of some sort,
and, as ever, I am sure, so much else
I am no longer able to remember.

Approaching My Sixty-third Birthday

So quiet,   waking from a nap,
not moving,   silence almost palpable
as if it were a presence,
as if it were to speak, to tell me something,...

and why remember anything, why now
that kiss?
Why of all kisses   is it the one I recall -
some thirty years ago,
right on my mouth,
a year and more before his death?
A premonition?

Maybe.

I don't recall my father ever kissing me before -
right on the mouth -
and there I was
hand out to shake his -
my father's kiss
as if to leave me something,
or was it just impulse,
or...
or what?

I don't know.

I remember nothing,   nothing of the rest of that evening.
I don't even remember seeing him again
before the viewing.

How was I to know?
Wherever,   silence fills me so.
Floorboards, stairs creak; my wife starts coming down.
Soon she will look for me.

And I?

Not far,   not more than a call away.

Last August

Don't bother asking about last August,
washed away in the rain,
covered by snow.
Last August, a swirl of blueberry picking,
impromptu outings, all day hiking,
and one last go at swimming in the lake,
and nameless things closer than distant
in the lengthening shadows.
But later were there not geese overhead,
deer foraging just off the trail,
and far into the night, keeping us awake,
human voices, dogs barking,
ORV's in the distance,
and closer by an engine, a motorcycle's, being revved up,

and were we not exhausted wondering about the next day
and the next putting today behind us,

and were we not,

were we not like the drift of clouds,

clouds,
            ordinary and passing.

Sighs and Stray Gusts

Waving goodby,

waving to myself,   my past,
slowly turning over

waving into my own slow turning over,

waving further,

overhearing my own memory,
my own sighing
over grass, crushed apples, bear scat,
or immeasureable waves in Tranquility Bay;

waving away harbinger of dampened fires,
insousciant tirades, metashivers
resuscitated on hearing
the last bird of winter,
a blind owl hooting, cat meowing;
unwavering departure,
unable to stop waving goodbye,
dyslexia in gesture;
that blind owl hooting, memory teeming
with endless successions of waving goodby,
slowly revolving into tropical tropes,
iridescent featherings,

waving goodby
slowly turning into road kill, scattered carcasses,
bayous of gratuity, tide drift,
uncensored trials scattering the demimondes of sacrifice
the extraneous subsequently dilutes,

slowly waving goodby.
Can error, virtue refract the pagan light?
Caramels dissolve, stairwells revolve.
Slowly treading moving stairs
who is it that waves,

what winds through the tall grass?
And what will the catkin, samara do?

The sanddollar at my feet, the water's recession,
an early morning light offer no clue,
no finality to waving.

I have seen no bespeckled egg in the rough grass.
Reeds mask the waters edge.
Semaphoric the slightest stirring of branches,
messages abound.

I have bantered with shadows, stray gusts,
and who has not waved turning away to other distractions,
misplaced wavering over,
misplaced waving off of, misplaced dollop of patience.

I have forgotten,

snippets and cobwebs,
dandelion bracelets.

Or waving, waiting for tomorrow. Whatever is met, evaded,
maddens the pace,
elongates the narrow, furthers the obtuse.
Marshaled, the dreaded trumpet,
spill marbles across the way,
the brown needled pines gesticulate,

what more could be said some flora turns,

signs.
What more? Among jasper,   aspen,   rivulets,
waving away inopportune thoughts,
waiving unprompted outcries, legacies,
hunched-over in forgetfulness,
a further turning from those that have died,

turning away,

waving,

waving giddily,

waving goodby.

After Looking at a Drawing by Albrecht Durer

No, no -

not this drawing,
this distant face,
not dislike
or turning away
or anything.

I can not count,
I can not estimate,
think

nothing,
not anything,
not this ninety-three year old man,
not one line,
one shading,

after almost five hundred years
of nothing -
face, head
that rested on his hand.

I can not think it,
can not escape,
not cling to it,
hold it -

not one line,
not one wrinkle, half-closed eyelids, quiet eyes
evade me,
not any of those ninety-three years

escape me,
not one.

I can not hold it.

On the Intertidal Rocks

And I would walk upon a distant beach,
absentminded,
hopscotching over footprints in the sand,
listening on the intertidal rocks,
listening to the ordinary,
sea surf and wind - and wind - on a rock covered shore.

And I would revel in sunlight,
watch it decompose in the prismatic spray,
lecture seagulls,
wash in,
                wash out,
in tidal play,
wander toward horizonal mirages
where the sand,
                beach,
the southern sun,
pounding waves meet,
and beached, pounded,
remember on the sandy dunes beach plums,
birdcries, and image shaking heat.

And I would hear an antique noise,
forgotten voice,
wayward in the sea breeze,
plucked instrument
partially heard and partially remembered.

And I would gather all that I had heard,
release it into the empyreal air -

let memory,

let mirage

disappear.

Thankless Summons

Having been there before,
found unfamiliar what should not have been;
faces, scenes twisted.
A termagant bristles at such things
and so the thankless summons.
A framework that offers no contest.
A blank to where I can not reach
and no reprise.

Yes, shadows completed the effect.
All the particulars that keep me going
are driven further and further:

and the red rocks by the sea,

and the tree tops touching,

and the dirt at my feet.

A Sometime Curmudgeon Spells Out His Brief

Enough! Enough of this cockatoo in spring.
Fetch me the March winds.
Align the bloomers on the clotheslines accordingly.
Smartly now, give an urchin's elephantine gasp
to poseurs; if you wish, revisit preteen demonology;
again, preserve orange hothouse scallions,
for there will be no reparations,
no contravening tomorrow's command,
only a noncommittal shrug
at each stranger's toppling into that lasting descent,
but no improprieties,

no guffaws   at each one's decent best.

Oh, can that
have I not heard the yawn from that puffed up beyond,
have I not heard the grunts, the squeals,

for what matters now is this cockatoo in spring,
these tart, these late arriving,
                        arabesque March winds.

Me! Me! Me!

Someone is hitting piano keys,
dots of explosive sound,
no numinous aura to
the moment's focus, to a particular piece of furniture,
to unstable atmospheric conditions,
and left are sleepless nights and fitful days,
a welling up of anger, rage.

The source?
The source could be me.

Me?

But, but I never tire of thee,
inexhaustible, a rise at every climax,
with thee nothing spoils but is always fresh,
whether it's my smelling coffee, my own laughter,
or a good colon emptying shit.

A fey doggy indecency rolling in my own deeds.

Sometimes I'm so taken
I fall in love all over again,
goose pimply from my slightest achievement.
I listen daily, all day,
pleased,
no sweeter laughter, no greater rectitude.

Irritated? Sometimes,
but not for long,
the very epitome of forgiveness.

How could I've been so lucky.
I can't imagine,
I just can't imagine what it would be like to be other than me.

Looking

Shouldn't be. Shouldn't be
palpitating flesh - emergency entrance, emergency action,
heart, lungs stopped for hours
as people cut and spliced and sewed
me up again. Now years and years have been -
white haired,   slowed pace,   laughter,
more to remember and less well remembered.
Looking at myself, looking elsewhere,

a dragonfly's path seems extreme,

rain falls and falls to an exacting measure.

Gouged

Fine! I, too,
once,
thereby, denounced,
remain.
Who did in who?
Strayed,
emptied of...,
guided by...,
quickly delivered.
Dwarfed by take-overs,
mistaken as loss.
When I look back
a snail is on my trail
adrift with lotus petals;
a hummingbird intercept
jostles my self-esteem.
Beyond,
crusted and old,
there, too, snowflakes leave me less sure;
again, stayed
but what was it
yet not germane?
Are all landscapes indifferent,
are any pertinent?
I could be collateral,
sun-flowered,
idyllic.
Not right, yes, not right, then.
Who ignores me
ignores a beast.
When was the last cock-a-doodle-doo,
the last latter day knockabout,
the last gouged out gain?

Among Others, Teddybears

Friends I have known.
It shall go no further.
How the past
has taken over,

controlled,
divided,
without relief in a letting go -
a life totaled.

A button missing,
acorns,
bunyans,
disparate feelings,
unhinged
small furtive playthings -
tedium's trinkets
holier than ennui
but not arousing as a Bengal tiger
or hoped for horses on the horizon,
or, even, vigorous walks that clarify.

I have known
objects implode,
processions turned away,
childhood, teddybears, uncontrollable laughter,
the irritability of a sullen face,
a solemn pledge,
unsought for events,
friends and having forgotten their names -
a private catalogue.

Only so much retained,
the rest whiffs of air
and stains upon a sidewalk.

A Day's Message

Incandescence shunted into cockiness,
ignored by fetid cockroaches, crab grass foragers,
realized in fragrant jasmine, in passion flowers,
fragmented in remembered mimosa,
remembered azalea garden,
or, on returning home,
in an hibiscus bloom in mid-winter in the backroom,
or in an unhappy cry over patterns ending in a shrug,
in twilight,
ending
in a poem.

No transcendent messenger this day,
passages terminating in a wispy cloud cover,
in a friable late afternoon sky.
Am I on a path,
am I being tracked?
The miscellaneous fills
each journey's journal,
the quickened flight of a blue jay,
a sloth's lethargic climb.
So much more could be said -
the suddenness of the accidental,
a mild hysteria on still existing,
a quieting of my breath
observing the cantilevered sweep of tasseled dried grass.

So many arrangements, so many ifs leave me woozy,
indiscriminately ignoring chance and fate,
whether stupified and/or pleased
by the smallest of words,
by the most protracted phrasing,
by each unsolicited incomprehensible look.

The tide, huge waves, sun dazzled surfaces,
relaxing in the warmth from the sunlight on one's face
are shelters from last thoughts,
a roiling cornucopia

of whispering and shouting,
a festive going out from under.

THREE

3/22/03

Someone has died and it is Saturday afternoon again

and it is the opera

and it is Desdemona

and, after radio, TV,
a seemingly inevitable progression.
There, there is smoke and fire from oil wells
and clouds of dust from far away tanks
and APCs and arcane explosions
and crowds filling streets
and placards protesting
and placards supporting

and soon another today will take this one's place
almost as if it had never been
almost a hidden trauma, a likeness lighter than air,

like lovers in a lattice of light

like a never heard eerie call of a jaguar

like the supposed furtive presence of a coyote

like some relief other than liquor, drugs, or prayer,

or never other than variants of toxic shock
never other than a shaggy maned frothy mouth
than a separated shoulder
than a split finger nail
than an adolescent's shrug
than throngs coming together and milling about
than being shat upon
than the start of chronic pain
than being unable to sing
and in the midst of it the enormity of detail
the inferential indifference to loss

the huge blank slack between memories

the waywardness of each moment

the prophetic denial of prophecy

the languid lording it over others
jeopardized in the on going rush of tomorrow

the green gross crackling of yesterdays

and a summery summons to a tiny fitful sleep.

Anonymous

If I had lived...
if there had been a death camp
where I had lived,
if...

living there
beside a death camp,
would it have been safe
and how safe could that have been
and would one have worried much,

living beside a death camp?

Anonymous, the living - wisely, then.
Ebullient, as ever,
                         greeting friends.

If I had lived...
would it have been any different
in any routine
living beside a death camp,
a heightened sense
of living,
surviving,
living beside a death camp,
a heightened sexual appetite,
any appetite,
living beside a death camp,
and would there not have been
the usual, inexplicable exaltations

of being,
of living,
living beside a death camp?

If I had lived
beside a death camp....

Anonymous, the living - wisely, then.
Ebullient, as ever,
                    greeting friends.

Would I have done
anything
living beside a death camp?
And wouldn't anything have been foolish?
Anything?
Would I have died
living beside a death camp?
Would I
in anger, in protest, communion

have died
living beside a death camp?

Anonymous, the living - wisely, then.
Ebullient, as ever,
                    greeting friends.

If I had lived...
would I have been bothered,
put upon,
living beside a death camp?
Would I have grumbled
over stenches, over boxcar
arrivals, departures,

morning,
          noon,
                    night,
sighing, rolling my eyes?
Would I?
Would I have bothered to have noticed
if I had lived
beside a death camp?

Anonymous, the living - wisely, then.
Ebullient, as ever,
                    greeting friends.

If I had lived
noticing nothing,
noting that there was nothing to notice,
nothing out of the ordinary,
no dailiness disturbed,
routine altered,
nothing,
how would I have been bothered
living beside a death camp?

Anonymous, the living - wisely, then.
Ebullient, as ever,
                    greeting friends.

If I had lived
addressing you in the local bar
worrying aloud as to where it would all end....

If I had not lived
beside a death camp
would it have mattered

if I had not?
Would it have changed me
and could it have mattered whether it changed me or not
if I had not
or if I had

lived beside a death camp,
anonymously,
alongside my shadow, myself?

And who would have worried when winter came,
and who when shadows fell,
when darkened,
            lightless,

            flowers failed,

living beside a death camp?

If I had not lived
or if I had

beside a death camp....

Anonymous, the living - wisely, then.
Ebullient, as ever,
                    greeting friends.

Leveller

Edging towards zero,
towards cipher,
turning
over soil, manure,
turning
over self,
turning
into another
unheralded
        fractious
            leveller.

Help!

Help, whoever.

Not to have scurried,
dropped whatever it was,
hurried?

Not help
wherever
careful
confronted
found

fractious

found

unheralded
        dumb
           leveller?

Remembering Some Verses by Pablo Neruda

I too have lived so much.

My heart was also inexhaustible

but who among those nameless names inscribed on stone
in each one's local cemetery
had not lived, not lived so much,
or whose heart was not inexhaustible,
or of those paupered, massacred, buried in mass graves,
of one among them
who had not lived so terribly hard,
who had not gone beyond exhaustion,
who had not exceeded his own implacable self,

or how this earth is littered
with the bones of the inextinguishable.

Hidden ruins, keepsakes,
compost for an enchanted disaffected bloom,
tag-tailed disjointed memories,
toenails that never stop growing.
Oh, those erasers taken out and banged together,
chalk settling on the sidewalk.
Some final residue of letters,
epistolary pasts
hosed down the drain,
blown by the wind,

caught on the soles of shoes.

Will this not end non sequiturs?
But wait,   for only mention wind,
a flying jib,   ripped sheets,
or next door, shots,
distorted shouts,

elbows out to pass,

the waywardness of crowds,

large numbers jostling each other.

All manner of having lived,

of having lived so much,

of talking it up upon getting together,

to have elaborated

with all the customary   congratulatory sighs

on how the heart is inexhaustible -

and, yes, yes,   at the end,   to have remembered it.

Rub-a-dub-dub

Blues, bambino,
pucker up.
Let recapitulate recapitulate.
Don't pick.
Sore's ache shall greet
feathery touch,
yellow tarnish into grief
reviving musty sentiments.

Inter your treasured phrasings
less helplessness be hostage to belief
or white be keening, red

imposter to possessing.
The lightest foot deaf
no further brightness fills.
No one comes out to play,
brown darkening to termagant, to faded...,
warmed-over rage.

Endure?

And my you're sure
yo-yoing spats to hunger pangs.
Sheer off of cabal of celestial slights,
swear off complicity.

Rub-a-dub-dub, honey,
parlay it into malarkey,
stuff and further considerations,

consigned to the arcane,
testy,
        touchy..., junkyard

for the sublime.

Tenets of Being

Display? Dogs straining at their chains.
The varied flower pots, hung tapestries,
banana bread. Concoctions of orange bread,
strawberry bread. Oh, let him be, crass purveyor,
cuddling confections of dubious origin; let him be
maker of his own statements, cherish
his left over lemon peels, watch him, sifter in hand,
cull over yesterday's menus; again, let him be,
smiling apace, winking at the mirror,
a veritable bonanza of good will,
an opener and closer: doors, chit-chat, etcetera.
A furtherance of angels could no more distill
his topsy-turvy well-being,
or better the moth beating its one free wing
being put out-of-doors,
or on a road's edge,
escorting - cars veering toward the center -
a caterpillar humpety, humpety crossing.
And still that raucous crying of the angelic host
not even presentiments of age could quell.
But then who could have known?

Peddle thy wares elsewhere!
Out of warehouses tippity toeing,
he will not be sequestered,
nor accept rebuke, no matter how grave your manners.
So what sags, sags;
let wrinkles be.
Macaws should snort at such tomfoolery.
Sanitize the multitudinous paths of grace.
Restructure space.
Oh, reconsider terrestrial beginnings.
What wraiths there are
in cushiony positions.
And no deliverance from most uprightly holding forth.
Have you not heard -
and not tra-la-la-la, either -
of that elaboration of sound Mrs. Verdunk is so famous for?

How the basses tremble.

Troupers to the fore,   modest,   impeccable,
galvanizing grains of sand, molten yellow.

Oh no, to be outdone,
and yes, quixotic trials, lapidary
archaisms of today's vernacular, colloquies of intent,...

bitter greens for the home-makers of tomorrow,...

nor care to drape what could have been on any backseat,...

so salutations to the least belief, to the gatherer of stars
moving upon the waters.

Lest it be forgotten,
cheers for the company of the dutiful,
carriers of weathered dreams,
unperturbed lancing shafts of light,

queuing up, patiently,
kibitzing as to the improbable.

Minute Particulars

The next compensates and the next.
Who 's whistling with or without teeth,
whose steamed greens can partially allay,
whose curried green tomatoes can be said
to cater to contentment?
So, minute particulars do tell.
A small breeze ruffles my hair,
curtains blown about,
Mary's inability to mount,
night disengaged,
a mix of satisfaction and pleasure
in eating early small budding sulphur shelves -
no,
not appropriate,
nor is a spectral glow,
a warbling euphony,
or racketing melange of elbows and kneecaps,
a distancing hello,
a transient haunting refrain,
a gesture that can't be recalled.
As for the embossed anecdotal, maybe,
maybe not,
with brother, father following one another
in partially remembered, memorable lives.

Car bombs, obscenities
exchanged at each street corner,
walls of flame, then,
who would not be taken aback,
quieted,
by each dereliction,

each escape,

each unaffordable mishap.

Where To Go

To start,
whose part remembered?
What was encountered?
Was it promise,
patterns reinstated,
a loss borne,
balustrades repeated?
The sly clipped, wheedled
by shadowy felons,
belligerant to being bettered,
tapped as overhead.
Slackers drifting caught
in vortical vertexes,
in time-lapsed corners.
Estranged, bartered, departures that were not to be denied.
And those flowers, red-purple, and that dissent;
who now remembers noble sentiments -
enraptured, quasi-honest?
Decorative then simple,
a blaze
haphazardly claimed
transited then to trains, peregrines.
Enough!
Not iridescent,
not final emblazoning -
burnt matchsticks, dirty handkerchiefs,
used tampons,

that no one, but no one,
could think of counting.

FOUR

Jade

Bead spangling bead,
particular pitted to particular,
patriarchial in upheaval,
luxuriate diamonded forests,
emeralded escapades,
jadal illumination illuminating
were not meant to be remembered.
Jade, gold
cauterized at noon
remembered
to be held,
protected,
glowing
through the latest
of the late afternoons.

Jade cutting gold,
green spotted yellow,
emeraldine hush of water
were not meant to be remembered.
Titanic,
metallic
honeycomb at noon,
yellow speckled green,
the least thing
remembered,
remembered
best
at noon,
was not meant to be remembered,
was not
gold mixed with green,

was not
jade, emerald,
irreparably gold

remembered
best
as noon
as sun
dwindling into the west,
was not meant to be remembered,
was not
jade consequent to jade,
was not the latest afternoon,
that late strip of westward orange,
night turning further into night,
black transfigured, crushed, to black.

Knockabouts and Pogo Sticks

Scuttled.
calypso shunned.
And so to find
night captioned, the largest
longed for
reduced.
Who was to be pleased?

Someone's surrogate, feisty,
unpardonable
as jerry-rigged templates
calling out to each.
a seizure, gloss, and frame
that came out of nowhere;
longing that knew no complaint.

a billowing belled
yellowing surfeit of clouds
repeated
til crimson dashed;

fragmented, seized,
not to have been released;
completed by someone's hair blown back -
left quirky straight, a tightening without relief.

As, usual, things: some knockabouts, those pogo sticks.

Remember, for once, lace, vulnerable and frayed,

a window just so,

a vase of wilted lilies, dead flies on a dusty floor,

sandalwood and, barely visible, someone else's bare foot.

Evening, Hound Dogs, and Rain

Play on,
more
than stay,
maybe.
Not hastily
as when tendered,
tampered with.
A gondolier sings,
a gemstone fitted,
to arms, such as they are.
The least no longer gallant
must have had it -

as something flows
rendering on
onto onward.

The littlest recorded
and the singing and the charm
and the parades and the washed out homes
and then an almost unheard of closure.

Hound dogs again,
and the rain and windowpanes;
and succeeding and
and not contained.

But, oh, those worms,
wriggling, ill-fated
when hunted,

but not one humbled,

not one
discarded.
Back to hound dogs
conceding nothing
that could not be retained,
and, and, and,

measureable,
yet, ephemeral as evening.

The Pitiless Complained

Had been

just as before;

so partial,
explorer of oneself,
solicitor, too.

Minimally -

toadstools? Ferns?
Yes, incoherently
concerned.

Not easy
but rarely capped.

The toothless cared.

The blind refused.

Neither would be had.

Put off?
Scared? No, devout.

Address
dark
darkening
an antique terror.

The pitiless complained.

No matter how distraught,
others prayed.

Continent After Continent

First, fatigue from waiting,
sorting out the nuances of patience,
proprieties of syntax suggest indefinite delay;
clay figurines, painted terra-cotta, innumerable
blue pin-striped double breasted suits, bells
tolling, then, one further tally of yesterdays.

Wasn't it a dream where somebody pointed out
bird droppings on my cheek?
Weren't there lovers reunited,
a solemn feast, choristers,
breezes reminiscent of spring?
Yet, there was fatigue,
blatant impatience, notes
passed back and forth in an angular calligraphy,
the toll of fullness in abbreviated afternoons.
Throughout the empty square unfiltered sunlight,
suspended dust falling,
rising, the thickening air.
Pale hunger,
tomorrow's anger
coalesce,
lips press together.
Abrasive monotonic voices sulk
over each wayward act,
charge the least soiling with malfeasance.
Petulance in a stranger's look
and a slow walk toward danger
past jewel scarabs,
elephants cocking their ears,
tropical ranges,
unmapped continents of a florid, unsettled self.

Exuberant

Skin tight Levi's,
last vanity of youth's escapades,
last gesture
of a greater would be nobility,
of crescendo
following crescendo,
towards a day's disintegration,
a robin's manifesto,
a chipmunk's pause,
unrequited
novel
sexual assignments.
Who is to hunt for the secret narrative
of each person's life,
each intractable animal?

Whether it was lunch, dinner, or sleep,
a music of soundless entreaties
that came after
with its own affect.
Stairs that vanished as we descended.
Stairs, music,
an autumnal patina spreads -
a child's shrill cry,
a huge fear,
a lasting deficit.

A flute player without a flute
on the far side of an empty square,
the far side of each glance,
and the fartherest side of a paradisical thought
serenely composed as a kitten falling
landed upright.
The flute player is no longer there,
then, reappears,
gesticulating to the images of another era,
to an unfolding light;
and out of the explicit shadows
to have found

there past the outlying hills and lowering fog,
sun turned, heightened, held
bronze, purple, yellow, white,
intoxicated
further than the plush exuberance of blooming peonies,
those who may have been the fulfillment of a final
magnificence.

Unconstrained In or Out of Season

Dehydrated,
deloused,
then, less than before.
Water trickling through impurities,
edges blurring,
phantoms reappearing,
a trapezoidal illusion.
Those blue shadows, white curtains
that the wind blows about
and the least aperture
sparkling in a crystalline coda
of nostalgia and unforgettables
as the wind, cold, and snow
can render one out of season,
conscious of honeysuckle, buttercup,
even, a bumble bee,
even, an elapsed valediction,
and one truncated memory of a day before any other,
of a yes
and, then, a no,
a chickadee forwarding itself,
and that robin's swagger,
that partially hidden worm that may or may not be devoured -
what light lights in its indifference.
The magistrate of tomorrow's griefs,
always capricious,
always irresolute,
chattily lascivious today as he well
might have been yesterday
ignores
chintzy silverware replaced by even chintzier,
by reconstructed Mobius strips,
and how much longer discordant discontinuities,

unlikely linkages, unlabelable poetry,
or how much longer this runny nosed,
irreverent me

adamant, at least, for a while, on being.

As To Far Away

A fitful closing down, shrouded furniture,
drapes in disarray,
frosted windows
and a shadowy vestibule.
Distressed by such stale air
contretemps and aliases
disappear
as in a dream, apprehensive,
getting nowhere,
as a spider pauses overhead.

Another morning, another fact,
the music of the dead,
a rhythmic displacement
sanctified; descendents eclipsed,
continuing to weep, tinnitus as myth,
and as to far away
to have gone even farther than that.

A Memory But of What?

Sailless,
broken mast,
drifting,
an albatross floating overhead.
A day no one, no one will remember,
waves rocking the boat,
shirtless,
sun-dissed,
sweating,
bemused gaze
with nothing to look at but distance.

How Goes The Day

They flow from something
crooked, scuttled,
resistant to smirking.
Incurable,
notwithstanding;
mirrors of each other's mirage.
Capped, rebutted;
a caption that may be of nothing,
a torque,
an invention,
a whorl of a whirling cascading
effervescent bubbling,
divested, contrary,
and bursting.

They flow from something.

**For All Those Whom Gustav Klimt Painted: Adele
Bloch-Bauer I,
Emilie Floge, Mada Primavesi, Fritza Riedler, Unnamed
Models,
Et Al.**

Too much -
too much gold, luster,
too much design, ornateness,
too much myself,
extended, touched,
inundated by each cluster
of gold, of purple,
of heightened color.
Crumpled vermillion lovelier...,

nor pair of scuttling claws, nor razor.
Nowhere
ground cover,
dull, dying vegetation,
amorphous
ground color,
plaintive - glossed over.

Each of you
has been held,
each
pictured
at least once,
each
held dearer - dresses
dyed heightened color,
dyed purple,
dyed gold,
dyed vermillion,
dyed lovelier... -
held
at least once,
each
caught,
fixed,

a calculated figuration -
neither significant nor trivial.

Each face,
if complacent...
if willful...
displayed,
seen -
a flowery pistil arrangement -
whether ductile...
whether brittle...

final -
as any fortuitous,
           winding sheet scene.

Walking Out

The beastly walk and walk:
walk out into the nightly air
the daily fire
indifferent weather
the crying out of bird

carried by wind

carried further

a crying in the night

a child

loose feathers -

fretful

worried.

www.ingramcontent.com/pod-product-compliance
Lightning Source LLC
LaVergne TN
LVHW091207080426
835509LV00006B/872